# Shalu
# Diwali, the Festival of Lights

## by NICK SHARMA

**PENMAN**
PRODUCTIONS

PO Box 400
Gleneden Beach, Oregon 97388
penmanproductions.com

*Shalu, Diwali, the Festival of Lights*

FIRST EDITION

Penman Productions, Gleneden Beach, Oregon
Copyright © 2016 Nick Sharma

All rights reserved under International and Pan-American Copyright Conventions.

No part of this publication may be reproduced, stored in a retrieval system,
or transmitted in any form by any means, electronic, mechanical, photocopying,
recording, or otherwise, except brief extracts for the purpose
of review, without written permission of the publisher.

The events, people, and incidents in this story are the sole product of the author's imagination.
The story is fictional and any resemblance to individuals living or dead is purely coincidental.

Printed in the United States of America

Library of Congress Control Number: 2015952364

ISBN: 978-09914804-4-9

Cover art, interior illustrations by Marek Szal
Book layout and cover design by Suzanne Fyhrie Parrott
Headshot photo of Nick Sharma by Innis Casey

Inside front cover art from © Canstock Photo Inc:
Tatiana53 / "Stock Photo - Globe. 3d. India"

Services provided in the United States
Printed by Penman Press

P.O Box 400, Gleneden Beach, Oregon 97388
www.PenmanProductions.com

*Dedication*

*This book is dedicated to
my mom and brother
who are my guiding light
and always there for me
to return home to whenever
the world gets dark.*

*~Nikku*

# Contents

*"Diwali, the Festival of Lights"* story

About the Tradition

When is the Diwali Festival?

Do you know what these words mean? (activity)

Learn Hindi: words and their meaning

What to do if you get lost

Important Information to Know

About the Author

"During Diwali, we celebrate by putting lots of little lights everywhere called Diyas. Diya's have small wicks like a candle and are usually inside a clay bowl that uses a special type of slow burning oil that lights like a candle—that's why people call it the Festival of Lights."

"We put lights up everywhere like the way people celebrate Christmas and then we wish for good things for everyone, like happiness, wealth and health!"

Shalu's brother and friend say goodbye to Shalu, but Shalu is too busy thinking of all the good things she can wish everyone for Diwali that she doesn't notice them leave.

When Shalu goes outside, she notices that it is already dark. Shalu doesn't like the dark.

The monster gets smaller as it walks out from behind the garbage cans. It's a little cat! Shalu laughs. It was just the cat's shadow playing tricks in the moonlight.

"You're not so scary," says Shalu to the cat.

Shalu finds her way home where everyone is waiting for her.

"Well, we are all happy you're safe, Shalu. I love you." Shalu's mother smiles.

"I love you too ma," says Shalu.

"Diwali is a celebration of lights but it's also a celebration of coming home and being with the people you love. So for this Diwali, I wish happiness, health, and love for you and your family. My name is Shalu and thank you for listening to my story. See you next time!"

## About the Tradition

**Diwali** is the Festival of Lights. It is a festival that runs for five days and celebrated all throughout India, as well as the world and is generally considered to be the largest Indian festival. Leading up to the festival people clean their houses, and prepare for the celebration. They even buy sweets and treats as well as gifts for each other to represent wealth and prosperity. It is like a birthday, Independence Day, and Thanksgiving all mixed into one. Although the reasons for celebrating Diwali are different from family to family, as well as area to area, the general celebration is the victory of Light over Darkness. Families celebrate this by putting lights throughout the house, as well as the streets using various methods such as electric lights, candles, wicks in clay bowls, and in general, anything that gives off light. And at night people light the skies with fireworks and displays of brilliant colors.

In the end, the festival of lights brings families together worldwide to celebrate together in love and harmony and take a moment to shine the light that is hidden inside all of us. **Happy Diwali!**

# When does Diwali Festival?

*Diwali is a five day festival that starts on different days each year.*

**2016** Sunday, October 30

**2017** Thursday, October 19

**2018** Wednesday, November 7

**2019** Sunday, October 27

**2020** Saturday, November 14

**2021** Thursday, November 4

**2022** Monday, October 24

**2023** Sunday, November 12

**2024** Friday, November 1

**2025** Tuesday, October 21

# Do you know what these words mean?

**Namasté**

**Celebration**

**Location**

**Brilliant**

**Landmark**

**Prosperity**

**Harmony**

*Answers on page 35.*

# Learn Hindi

Hindi is one of the top five spoken languages in the world! Because of the large number of people and areas it is spoken, there are many different dialects and variations of Hindi. Here are just some words to help you learn a little bit of Hindi.

There are many words for **Light** in Hindi. Some are: **Prakash, Gatti, Jyoti** and **Diya**

**Din** is the Hindi word for **Day**.

**Rat** and **Rajani** are Hindi words for **Night**.

**Aag** and **Agni** are the Hindi words for **Fire**.

**Pani** is the Hindi word for **Water**.

**Svasthy** is the Hindi word for **Health**.

**Khoya, Gum** and **Gumarah** are Hindi words for **Lost**.

**Mili** and **Paaya** are Hindi words for **Found**.

# Do you know what these words mean? (answers)

**Namasté** is a customary greeting that is a common way of saying hi or hello. Namasté is often performed with the gesture of holding the hands together and slightly bowing the head down.

**Celebration** - A time to throw a party or do something special for a person or an event. Usually, a gathering of many people who have fun together like a birthday party.

**Location** - Where some place exists.

**Brilliant** - A word to describe bright and shining.

**Landmark** - A word for something such as a big building or a thing that stands out in its surroundings.

**Prosperity** - A word to describe success.

**Harmony** - A word that means to get along peacefully.

If you are together with other kids, make sure that you stay together.

# *Important Information to Know...*

Remember your name and a way to contact family in case of emergencies.

*Do you know your full real name?*

Full Name: _____

*Do you know your mom or dad's phone number?*

Phone Number: _____

*Do you know anyone else's phone number you can call in case of an emergency?*

Name: _____

Phone Number: _____

*Do you know where you live?*

_____

_____

Good work! Now keep this book with you in case of emergencies and remember to always be safe. My name is Shalu, and I will see you next time!

## About the Author

Nick Sharma is the author and creator of the popular Shalu Series. Nick is a novelist, poet, artist, screenwriter, and a former actor who currently lives in the United States. He has worked with large corporations such as Coca-Cola, Mercedes, and Intel for his talent. He began writing books, under the tutelage of Professor Ron Lovell, who has written over 26 books and textbooks, and who has also worked with large publications such as Business Week.

Nick formally signed with Professor Lovell and his company, Penman Productions, when he wrote his first novel, *How to be a Hero*, which was one of his original screenplays. He brought ground breaking storytelling, emotion, metaphors, and breathtaking imagery to his works and has been considered by various educational institutions for use within the classroom. Since then, Nick has written several books that have gotten into mainstream distributors such as Barnes and Noble and has been invited to lecture at various colleges, educational institutes, programs, and literacy centers.

Today, he continues to write about the world and the many wonders it has to offer, all the while educating the reader through his stories.

All Nick's work can be found at PenmanProductions.com including information about Shalu and his other children's books.